MADRID
THE CITY AT A GLANCE

C000277192

Círculo de Bellas Artes
This grand arts centre stands
to the groovy nightlife district
in for a coffee in the 1920s café or enjoy a
free classical concert at midday on Saturdays.
See p015

Arco de la Victoria
This triumphal arc was built by architect
Arregui in 1956 to celebrate the victory
of Franco's Nationalist army over the
Republicans during the Spanish Civil War.

Telefónica Building, Gran Vía
The first of several mini-skyscrapers to shoot
up around Gran Vía in the 1920s as Madrid
looked to adopt a Manhattan-style skyline.

Plaza Mayor
A proud, equestrian statue of King Felipe II
stands in the centre of this majestic, 17th-
century square. It's an important landmark
and a must-see for the first-time visitor.

Centro de Arte Reina Sofía
This former hospital was converted into one
of the city's seminal art museums in 1986. The
rather drab exterior has now been jazzed up
with a bulbous red extension by Jean Nouvel.
See p046

Plaza de la Paja
One of the few remnants of medieval Madrid,
this square was once used by the city's
bishop to auction off straw (*paja*) and is now
the playground of the city's beautiful people.

Palacio Real
For much of its 250-year history, this palace
was the seat of the Spanish monarchy. Its
countless treasures are testament to the
country's phenomenal post-imperial wealth.

INTRODUCTION
THE CHANGING FACE OF THE URBAN SCENE

The Spanish capital is on course for expansion, economic growth and an exciting flourish of creativity not seen since the post-Franco euphoria of La Movida Madrileña in the 1980s. While Barcelona became a global destination when it hosted the 1992 Olympics and has since become saturated with EU émigrés and tourists, giving it a superficial veneer of glamour, Madrid's allure runs deeper and its development has been far more organic.

Its three world-class museums, the Prado (Paseo del Prado, T 91 330 2800), the Centro de Arte Reina Sofía (see p045) and the Thyssen-Bornemisza (see p042), were all given extensions recently, simply because their collections had grown so vast that there was no more room to house them. And over the last decade the city has seen a massive upsurge in hip restaurants, bars and clubs to satiate the evolving tastes of its globe-trotting citizens. Plus its kicking nightlife, immortalised by film director Pedro Almodóvar, suits all tastes and budgets and beats Barcelona's hands down.

Thanks to the addition of a state-of-the-art terminal at Barajas Airport (see p073), the city has also become a global hub for South America and its increased capacity has seen slick designer hotels opening in every district. But this is a city where you're unlikely ever to feel that its culture is being stifled by an influx of foreigners, for behind the grand, imperial façade of this vibrant metropolis, you will always find the very soul of Spain.

ESSENTIAL INFO
FACTS, FIGURES AND USEFUL ADDRESSES

TOURIST OFFICE
Centro de Turismo de Madrid
Plaza Mayor 27
T 91 588 1636
www.munimadrid.es

TRANSPORT
Car hire
Avis, *T 91 393 7222*
Hertz, *T 91 393 7228*
Metro
T 90 244 4403
www.metromadrid.es
Taxis
Radio Taxi Independiente
T 91 405 1213
Radio Taxi Asociación Gremial
T 91 447 5180
Radio Teléfono-Taxi
T 91 547 8200

EMERGENCY SERVICES
Ambulance
T 112
Police
T 091
24-hour pharmacy
Canal de Farmacia
Calle de Mayor 13
*T 098 for daily list (or check
a local newspaper)*
www.canaldefarmacia.com

CONSULATES
British Consulate
Paseo de Recoletos 7 and 9
T 91 524 9700
www.ukinspain.com
US Consulate
Calle Serrano 75
T 91 587 2240
www.embusa.es

MONEY
American Express
*International Arrivals, Terminal Four,
Barajas Airport*
T 91 393 8216
www10.americanexpress.com

POSTAL SERVICES
Post Office
Plaza Cibeles
T 91 396 2733
Shipping
UPS
T 90 288 8820
www.ups.es

BOOKS
Fortunata and Jacinta by Benito Pérez
Galdós (Cambridge University Press)
**Madrid: A Cultural and Literary
Companion** by Elizabeth Nash
(Interlink Books)

WEBSITES
Art
www.museoprado.es
www.museothyssen.org
Newspapers
www.negocios.com
www.larazon.es

COST OF LIVING
Taxi from Barajas Airport to Centro
€25
Cappuccino
€1.10
Packet of cigarettes
€2.75
Daily newspaper
€1.50
Bottle of champagne
€29.50

MADRID
Area
600 sq km
Population
3 million
Currency: euro
€1 = £0.70 = $1.20
Telephone codes
Spain: 34
Madrid: 91
Time
GMT +1

Paris

Madrid   Barcelona

SPAIN

AVERAGE MAX TEMPERATURE / °C

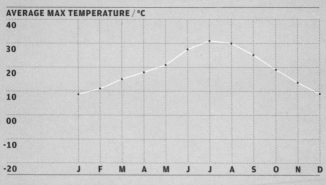

AVERAGE RAINFALL / MM

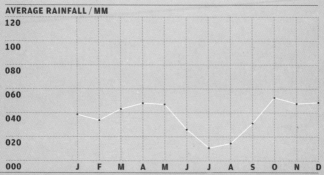

NEIGHBOURHOODS

THE AREAS YOU NEED TO KNOW AND WHY

To help you navigate the city, we've chosen the most interesting districts (see the map inside the back cover) and underlined featured venues in colour, according to their location (see below); those venues that are outside these areas are not coloured.

SALAMANCA

The sartorially elegant avenues of this district are home both to the city's upper classes (known locally as *pijos*) and the city's media, with gleaming boutiques of international luxury brands and up-market eateries hosting power lunches.

CASTELLANA

The Paseo de la Castellana is a leafy, multi-lane boulevard bracketed by skyscrapers — the city's financial centre. Nestled among the offices are small artistic gems, such as the home of Spanish artist Joaquín Sorolla and the Open Air Sculpture Museum, while beyond the leaning KIO Towers is the city's titan of design hotels, Puerta América.

CHUECA

Once the hub of Madrid's gay community, Chueca has since become a playground for all the city's youth, regardless of sexuality, and every week another trendy boutique, funky bar or chic, cheap restaurant opens its doors. The area really comes into its own, though, in late June/early July when Gay Pride attracts two million party-goers.

MALASAÑA

In the 1980s, the artistic, cinematic and literary movement La Movida Madrileña started here — judging by the bars, clubs and shops catering to punks, mods and rockers, it is still a mecca for alternative lifestyles. It's also home to the popular shopping street of Calle Fuencarral.

CENTRO

The 19th-century half-moon plaza Puerta del Sol is a favourite meeting point for many Madrileños. Just a few streets away, the magnificent, cobbled Plaza Mayor is testament to the might of one of the most powerful empires that the world has ever seen. Further south, El Rastro flea market has become a Sunday ritual for locals.

LAVAPIÉS

Jean Nouvel's bulbous red extension to the Centro de Arte Reina Sofía is the gateway to Lavapiés, a working-class area starting to feel the affects of gentrification now that neighbouring La Latina has become prohibitively pricey. Worth a visit for its cutting-edge galleries and the avant-garde performances at the Teatro Valle-Inclán.

LA LATINA

The sloping, leafy Plaza de la Paja right at the heart of La Latina has become the playground of Madrid's beautiful people in the last five years, particularly after midday on Sundays when brunch is the grand finale of a weekend cavorting around the city's legendary club scene.

RECOLETOS

The Paseo del Prado, punctuated by three fountains of the gods Apollo, Neptune and Cybele, is the Eastern border of the cultural and historical steeplechase of Recoletos. Anyone suffering from museum fatigue can find solace in the elegant El Retiro park.

LANDMARKS

THE SHAPE OF MADRID'S SKYLINE

Chances are your first impression of Madrid will be of the vaulted, undulating roofs and sci-fi spaces of Barajas Airport (see p073). Welcome to 21st-century Spain, where more concrete is now being poured than anywhere in Europe. The city limits are expanding with gleaming new suburbs, such as San Chinarro, and a new crop of contemporary landmarks – the Caixa Forum Madrid (Calle de Alameda and Calle de Almadén) by Herzog & de Meuron and El Matadero (Paseo de la Chopera 12, T 91 480 4968), a cultural complex housing the city's contemporary art collection, ARCO.

Declared the capital of Spain in 1561 by King Felipe II, Madrid's grand and austere façades in Centro, Recoletas and Salamanca were bankrolled by imperial gold and silver that poured in from Mexico and Peru. And while they may seem bland compared to refined Paris or modernista Barcelona, they are punctuated by architectural gems like the Palacio Real (Calle Bailén, T 91 454 8800) and the majestic Plaza Mayor. The arterial east-west avenue of Gran Vía is lined with small skyscrapers that heralded the 20th century and the fabulously retro Plaza de España was Franco's 1950s nod to the modernist movement. Then there's Torres KIO (Plaza Castilla), the leaning towers that declare the country's future economic ambitions with a rather audacious address, *Puerta de Europa*, 'the Gateway to Europe'.

For all addresses, see Resources.

Palacio de Congresos
This exhibition space along Madrid's
grandest avenue is hard to miss because
of the fabulous Joan Miró murals that
have become so much a symbol of the
city. Miró is also represented elsewhere
at the Open Air Sculpture Museum
(T 91 701 1863), where Calle de Juan
Bravo meets Paseo de la Castellana.
*Paseo de la Castellana 99, T 91 337 8100,
www.madridconventioncentre.com*

PALACIO DE CO

Torre Picasso

Originally designed by Minoru Yamasaki, the architect of the World Trade Center in New York, Madrid's tallest office building has a troubled history of its own. Work was originally suspended in 1984 when the original client, an explosives company, suffered financial meltdown and then the architect died. Eventually completed by Alas Casariego in 1988, it was built on a rigorous grid pattern and certainly makes an unmissable landmark towering over the whole city. It won't continue to have that distinction for long though, as the Torre Espacio skyscraper, in the Madrid Arena, will become the tallest in the city when Pei Cobb Freed & Partners' 220m-high block is complete.

Plaza de Pablo Ruíz Picasso

Teatro Valle-Inclán

The main square in Lavapiés now has a modern addition to its traditional, turn of the century architecture. Visitors arriving by metro are greeted by a boxy new build, the Teatro Valle-Inclán, which is becoming the centre for off-Broadway, avant-garde drama and theatre particularly pertaining to the Madrileño youth. It was built on the site of an old synagogue dating from the time when this was the centre of the Jewish ghetto. Lavapiés itself has always been a magnet for some of the more colourful of the city's denizens, including the famously militant cigarette girls, *à la* Carmen and the manolos, the lower-class dandies that were such a feature of Madrid.
Plaza Lavapiés, T 91 505 8800

Centro Colón

It might not be an especially handsome ornament to Madrid's central square, located just north of the vast Museo Arqueológico Nacional (T 91 577 7912), but it is hard to miss. These modern blocks of mostly offices and a kitsch waxworks museum that's probably best avoided make up the western side of the square. Across the way is the large verdant space of the Gardens of the Discovery and its cultural centre, located beneath the mysteriously powerful jet of water that shoots out from underneath the square's defining feature, its 1885 statue commemorating Columbus.
Plaza de Colón

Círculo de Bellas Artes

Once Madrid's answer to London's ICA and New York's Dia, the art at Círculo de Bellas Artes is now more Royal Academy summer show. The bar, however, is a retro 1920s treat – all marble busts and chandeliers floating beneath the stunning frescoes. The building itself is a soaring art deco pile designed in 1919 by Antonio Palacios, who also completed the city's robustly rococo post office. The tower, which helps to turn the Círculo into such a prominent landmark, was intended by Palacios as an urban lighthouse, illuminating the city.

Calle de Alcalá 42, T 91 360 5400, www.circulobellasartes.com

HOTELS

WHERE TO STAY AND WHICH ROOMS TO BOOK

For decades, Madrid's stately grande dame, the Hotel Ritz (Plaza de la Lealtad 5, T 91 701 6767), and belle époque The Westin Palace Hotel (Plaza de las Cortes 7, T 91 360 8000), both a stone's throw from the Prado, were simply the only options for diplomats, celebrities and fat cats looking for a temporary residence in the Spanish capital. In 1972, the Hotel Villa Magna (Paseo de la Castellana 22, T 91 587 1234) became something of an arriviste on the hospitality scene, luring in corporate heavyweights.

But the millennium heralded an unprecedented building boom in Spain which, coupled with the blossoming of nationwide design mania, has created a crop of new properties offering a thoroughly modern kind of hotel experience. Stately 18th-century palaces have been spruced up with contemporary furnishings and sleek interiors that belie their formal, classical facades to reflect the city's modern sensibilities. The Hotel Puerta América (see p028) may be seen by some as an architectural folly par excellence, but only in Madrid would a hotelier have the guts to commission a collection of the world's top-drawer architects and designers to leave their mark on one building. And just when we thought the city's deluge of new designer properties had peaked, we heard a whisper of yet more openings – there is even a new Hard Rock Hotel (Plaza de Santa Ana 14, T 91 531 4500).

For all addresses and room rates, see Resources.

Mario

The Hotel Campomanes, located just off Gran Vía, was always our favourite budget bolthole, thanks to its sleek design, perfect location and great rates. When it changed hands in 2003, new owner Room Mate kept the prices down, enlisted design maven Tomás Alía to update the interiors and added a new feature – each of the properties in its nascent chain represents the home of a sophisticated local. Mario was conceived as an urbanite who works in the music biz, hence the extensive library and 'music space', where guests can tune in to the latest tracks. With rates this low, we suggest you splash out on a Junior Suite or, if you're artistically minded, book into the Alicia (see p032), Mario's sister hotel. *Calle de Campomanes 4, T 91 548 8548, www.room-matehoteles.com*

Hotel Quo

Slick black and white architectural photos of some of Madrid's most iconic buildings add a sense of place to Hotel Quo, which, at 62 rooms, is the perfect size to ensure decent service. Located just steps from Puerta del Sol, it's the ideal pied à terre from which to explore the city. Tomás Alía chose a crisp, monochrome palette with touches of red for the rooms, such as in the Junior Suite (above), but his flare for creating inviting modern spaces is best displayed in the Salón Quo (left), where breakfast is served. We also like Superior Room 702, which has a jacuzzi bath and a terrace overlooking Calle de Alcalá. *Calle de Sevilla 4, T 91 532 9049, www.hotelesquo.com*

Vincci Soho

The discerning fashionista or art lover who doesn't have cash to splash would do well to check into a Standard Room (above) at the new Vincci Soho. The rooms and public spaces have real flair and all the city's major attractions are just a couple of blocks away. The bar lacks atmosphere and is not frequented by locals, but no matter – the happening Huertas nightlife district and seriously hip restaurant and bar Ølsen (see p064) are round the corner. If the Soho is full, try its sister property, Vincci Centrum (T 91 360 4720).
Calle de Prado 18, T 91 141 4100, www.vinccihoteles.com

Urban

Situated off Puerta del Sol, Urban has lent a touch of contemporary Gotham City-style grandeur to the Barcelona's epicentre. The huge vaulted steel-and-glass atrium (left) is impressive, despite the collection of nightmare-inducing Polynesian sentry-like statues. More sedate original ethnic antiques furnish the rooms, which are dark, broody and resolutely masculine; try the Royal Suite (above). The fifth floor has the best views, but make sure you master the baffling light switches and shutter controls before bedtime. Skip the roof terrace with its tiny pool, but do visit the Glass Bar and Europa Decó restaurant, a haunt of fashionistas and politicos, as the Loewe headquarters and Congress building are both nearby. *Carrera de San Jerónimo 34, T 91 787 7770, www.derbyhotels.es*

Palacio del Retiro

Capitalising on the wild success of the
Santo Mauro (see p036), AC Hotels
opened its second venture in 2004
in Madrid's cultural 'golden triangle',
a stone's throw from the three principal
museums. It combines the marble,
mouldings and stained-glass windows
of the original early 20th-century palace
(opposite) with contemporary mod cons
and furniture designed by the owner,
Antonio Catalan. Indice, the chic in-house
restaurant, has a modern Basque menu,
and the cocktail bar is an institution
among well-heeled locals. The 51 rooms
are pricey, but all have plasma screens,
state-of-the-art stereos and free minibars.
The nine suites, in particular the Luxury
Suites (above), have amazing views of
El Retiro park, a jacuzzi and a separate
reception area.
Calle de Alfonso XII 14, T 91 523 7460,
www.ac-hotels.com

Hotel Puerta América

It began life as a bland conference hotel, but thanks to the visionary head honchos at Hoteles Silken, it's become a testament to some of the greatest architects of the Noughties. Marc Newson's slick, high-ceilinged bar, John Pawson's beautiful, typically understated lobby (left) and Christian Liaigre's smart restaurant are just extraordinary public spaces. Jean Nouvel's take on global glamour pervades the top-floor suites, David Chipperfield and Arata Isozaki's rooms are monochrome and sleek while Ron Arad has designed seamless red pod units which incorporate bathroom, storage and a sexy circular bed dressed in black linen. Most spectacular of all is Zaha Hadid's first floor rooms (above), akin to Superman's glacial retreat. *Avenida de América 41, T 91 744 5400, www.hotelpuertamerica.com*

David Chipperfield's Floor, Hotel Puerta America

Alicia

Designer Pascua Ortega, locally acclaimed for Hotel Adler and the Teatro Real, has transformed an early 20th-century shoe factory into Alicia, the second Room Mate hotel in town (see Mario, p017). Ortega's inspiration for this hotel was the fictional hostess Alicia, an artist with a taste for fine dining and a host of celebrity pals, including art dealer Soledad Lorenzo, actress Leonor Watling and über-chef Sergi Arola. The lobby (above) is good example of Ortega's style. Museums and the verdant Jardín Botánico are a stone's throw from the elegant curved facade of Alicia's slick 'home' and all 34 rooms have plasma televisions and internet access. Duplexes 401 and 501 are best, thanks to their balconies and bathtubs with a view. *Calle del Prado 2, T 91 389 6095, www.room-matehoteles.com*

Hotel de Las Letras

Habitat Hotels has always gone that extra mile for its guests. At the Bauza (T 91 435 7545), Madrid's first design hotel, stereos are pre-programmed with more than 100 albums, there's an excellent library and free internet access, while latest venture, Hotel de Las Letras, has an excellent candlelit Catalan restaurant, a rooftop terrace and a lounge that has become a real fixture on the bar circuit of nearby Chueca. Decoration in the rooms, such as in the Standard Double (above), is inspired by quotes from the literary and arts world. If you plan to party until dawn, reserve a Plus Room with terrace. *Calle Gran Vía 11, T 91 523 7980, www.hoteldelasletras.com*

Roof terrace, Hotel de Las Letras

Santo Mauro

This seriously chic, 51-bedroom boutique hotel is a mecca for publicity-shy starlets and media magnets. Cutting-edge interiors and slick furnishings courtesy of Catalonian designer Josep Joan Pera complement the 19th-century opulence of this former residence of the Marqués de Santo Mauro (right), although the dark pool (above) lets the side down. Meanwhile chef Carlos Posadas directs an excellent seasonal menu in the restaurant housed in the impressive grand library. An atmosphere of discretion pervades the hotel's rooms, the old chapel and the verdant, walled 700 sq m garden, where the well-heeled conduct high-powered meetings. The hotel itself consists of the former palace and stables, we prefer the rooms in the Palacete Building, particularly Room 105 with its minimal aesthetic.
Calle de Zurbano 36, T 91 319 6900,
www.ac-hotels.com

Hotel Meninas

When local architects Ramón Caruz and Federico Somolinos converted an old, typical Madrileño apartment block set around a central patio into the Hotel Meninas they retained the *Melrose Place*-style vibe. The interiors are contemporary and cosy, see the lobby (left), although not a patch on the slick Mario (see p017), which has similar rock-bottom rates. If you're travelling en masse and don't mind bunking up, the suites are by far the best value as the two Junior ones sleep three each and the Suites Especial sleep up to four; the alternative is the Double Room (above). If the hotel is full, don't take up the offer of a room in sister property the Hotel Opera, but instead head over to Centro's Posada del Peine (T 91 523 8151). *Calle de Campomanes 7, T 91 541 2805, www.hotelmeninas.com*

24 HOURS

SEE THE BEST OF MADRID IN JUST ONE DAY

Madrid is renowned for its world-class museums, and a whizz around the vast collection at the Museo Nacional del Prado (Paseo del Prado, T 91 330 2800) is a must. Head for the Velázquez rooms, to admire his masterpiece of portraiture, *Las Meninas*, then move on to Goya's oeuvre, which ranges from delicate pastoral idylls and subtly satirical royal portraiture to the dark, nightmarish *pinturas negras* that he created after he went deaf.

For a more contemporary art tour, head for the Museo Sorolla (General Martínez Campos 37, T 91 310 1584), where some of the best canvases by Spain's impressionists are beautifully drenched in daylight. Take a turn around the Residencia de Estudiantes (Calle de Pinar 21-23, T 91 563 6411), where Lorca, Dalí and Buñuel met in the 1920s, then make your way to the Museo de Escultura al Aire Libre (Paseo de la Castellana 41, T 91 701 1863), an oasis of tranquility under a flyover below the Paseo de Eduardo Dato, for a picnic lunch among oversized works by great Spanish sculptors such as Chillida and Miró.

If you're visiting Madrid for some retail therapy, the city has all your heart might desire. And you could even enjoy a lightning-fast arts fix at the Centro Conde Duque (Calle de Conde Duque 9-11, T 91 588 5861) cultural centre between shopping strikes around Calle Conde Duque and Plaza Comendadoras.

For all addresses, see Resources.

10.00 Cacao Sampaka

Rock up to this mecca for chocaholics for a quick *cortado* (Spanish espresso), a fresh juice and a pastry or some toast smothered in their excellent own-brand jams. Then bulk-buy the slick gift boxes for a year's supply of birthday presents. The collections include gourmet truffles, which are allegedly favoured by the Spanish royals, liqueurs, dried fruits and nuts, spices from the Americas, *cocoas* (cheese-less pizzas from Mallorca), and the popular Single Bean Origins box. Only diehard fans of Ferran Adrià's culinary alchemy will love the weirder flavours, which include herbs, olives and anchovies. *Calle de Orellana 4, T 91 319 5840, www.cacaosampaka.com*

11.30 Museo Thyssen-Bornemisza

When the Spanish state bought Baron Thyssen-Bornemisza's outstanding art collection (the second largest private one in the world) in 1993, the Swiss were devastated to lose such a seminal body of work. Its current home, which completes the city's 'cultural triangle', has been given a slick new extension to show off yet more of its myriad treasures. Start on the second floor and hunt down Holbein's portrait of Henry VIII, Rubens' *The Toilet of Venus* and Breughel's *Garden of Eden*, then check out the expressionists (Shiele, Munch, Kandinsky and Otto Dix) on the first floor. Leave some time to linger on the ground floor, where 20th-century greats – Picasso, Pollock, Lichtenstein, Rothko, Bacon – command centre stage. *Paseo del Prado 8, T 91 369 0151, www.museothyssen.org*

13.30 Arola

For a leisurely lunch of Nordic fare head for Ølsen (see p064) to check out one of the trendiest new eateries in town. But if you're tight for time, keep on the cultural trail and refuel at the Reina Sofía's in-house restaurant to indulge in masterchef Sergi Arola's contemporary Spanish cuisine and soak up the splendour of Jean Nouvel's slick extension. The food is not of the standards of Arola's two-Michelin-starred La Broche (T 91 399 3437) or his eaterie in Barcelona's Hotel Arts (T 93 483 8065), but it is better priced and retains his signature flavours and flashy, artistic presentation.

Calle de Argumosa 43, T 91 467 0202, www.arola-madrid.com

16.00 Museo Nacional Reina Sofía

Ascend one of the two glass panoramic
lifts and make for the second floor where
Picasso's iconic monochrome *Guernica*
is the centrepiece in a series of galleries
devoted to his work. Adjacent are rooms
dedicated to Miró's cryptic canvases,
Calder's delicate mobiles, the sultan
of surrealism Dalí, and Kandinsky. The
fourth floor is equally impressive housing
Eduardo Chillida's abstract sculpture,

Anton Tàpies' obscure canvases created
from layers of found objects and work by
top-drawer international artists, including
Francis Bacon, Yves Klein, Henry Moore and
Lucio Fontana. Make sure you don't miss
Antonio Lopez's massive *Man and Woman*
sculpture in Room 31, surrounded on all
sides by beautiful landscapes of Madrid.
Calle Santa Isabel 52, T 91 774 1000,
www.museoreinasofia.es

22.00 Nueva Fontana

The three futuristic spaces here are the brainchild of designer Tomás Alía. Dine at one of the two restaurants (Azabara is more upmarket, while La Naveta specialises in seafood), but skip the club, Fontana, which is one of the flashiest in town but has a crowd consisting mainly of *pijos* (people who dress extravagantly). For a real insight into Madrid's cutting-edge clubland, head for Suite Cafe Club (see p067) or gothic club Le Ki (Calle de la Paz 5) for a night of Movida-style decadence and electronic, punk-rock and alternative music. On Thursdays, Flamingo at Franela Dance Hall (T 91 541 3500) is run by über-club-promoters Trip Family and is hugely popular with the trendy set. *Calle de Hernani 75, T 91 417 5693, www.lanuevafontana.com*

URBAN LIFE
CAFÉS, RESTAURANTS, BARS AND NIGHTCLUBS

Madrid's restaurants have become much more sophisticated in recent years, with design playing an increasingly important role. International and fusion cuisine are creeping onto the culinary scene and set lunch menus are a great way to sample many of the really chic establishments in town without blowing your budget. One excellent example is Teatriz (Calle Hermosilla 15, T 91 577 5379), the former theatre converted into a dramatic eaterie by Philippe Starck and Javier Mariscal.

While you're in town, one fancy traditional dinner is a must if only to dispel the myth that the local food tends towards the greasy and stodgy. If you like fish, make a reservation at La Dorada (Calle de Orense 64, T 91 570 2004), and for classic northern Spanish fare, book a table at Asador Donostiarra (Calle Infanta Mercedes 79, T 91 579 6264). Favoured by the city's fat cats, Lhardy (Carrera San Jerónimo 8, T 91 522 0731) is one of Madrid's smartest – and oldest – establishments, and looks much the same now as it did on the day that it opened in 1839. The renovated Club 31 (see p058) is another upmarket dining destination well worth a visit. If you're in search of really excellent tapas, head to Huertas, especially the bars around Jesús de Medinacelli church, or to La Latina – try the bull's tail and grilled courgette in Viuda de Vacas (Calle Cava Alta 23, T 91 366 5847).

For all addresses, see Resources.

Sopa

When jewellery and accessories designer Jorge Morales opened a shop in Jaime Arias' atelier in the trendy area of Ciudad Jardín, they both decided to combine heir passion for rings, necklaces and handbags, which are handmade for the likes of Paul Smith, with their love of organic food. The pair divided their industrial loft space into a deli selling treats such as almond mayonnaise, pepper jam, smoked goat's cheese, pasta, rice, juices and other kitchen staples, and a small restaurant serving homemade soups, sandwiches, ice creams and *cocoas* (Mallorcan cheese-less pizzas). Sopa has since become quite the fashionable lunch venue for creative types, despite its slightly odd location out of the city centre. *Calle de Nieremberg 23, T 91 413 1719, www.sopa.vg*

Fast Good

What does a world-class chef who's won every culinary accolade do next? Well, Ferrán Adrià of El Bulli (T 97 215 0457) fame has teamed up with NH Hotels to provide well-heeled Madrid with healthy, gourmet fast food. The menu includes green bean salad, gorgonzola burgers and french fries cooked in olive oil.
Calle de Padre Damián 23, T 91 343 0655, www.fast-good.com

Wagaboo

This exotic eaterie serving global cuisine is the latest creation of Madrid's premier restaurant designer Ignacio García de Vinuesa, who is also responsible for the interiors of Club 31 (see p058) and slick society Chinese restaurant Le Dragón (T 91 435 6668). The bare brick walls and exposed steel girders give Wagaboo an industrial feel, but García has made it more welcoming with wooden floors, bistro tables and a vibrant colour scheme of pale pink, deep red and black. The glassed-off kitchen serves Med-Asian specialities, plus a range of international dishes from Peruvian ceviche to Moroccan tagine. The set lunch menus are a complete snip – prices start at €8.95 and include a drink as well as either dessert or coffee. *Calle de Gravina 18, T 91 531 6567, www.wagaboo.com*

Bajó Cero

Argentine chain Giangrossi kick-started a craze for indulging in a late-night tub of dulce de leche ice cream washed down with a beer before bedtime (the most central eaterie is found on Calle de Alberto Aguilera 1, T 91 444 0130). We prefer a more exclusive establishment to round off an evening pigging out on chocolate chip and indulging in one last drink. Designer Tomás Alía, supermodel Nieves Álvarez and Argentine fashion designer Roberto Torreta have opened the perfect place in Bajó Cero, with 18 flavours of ice cream and fat-free sorbets, a selection of pastries and bottled beer. It's open until midnight on weekdays and 1am at the weekend.
Glorieta de Quevedo 6, T 91 445 3827, www.bajocero.es

Ojalá

From the people who brought us the modern tapas bar La Musa Latina (T 91 354 0255) comes Ojalà, a hip hang-out in the hot 'hood of Malasaña. In the evening, a louche crowd gathers in the chill-out space downstairs, which has cushions, a sand-strewn floor and walls lit up with projected visuals.
Calle de San Andrés 1, T 91 523 2747, www.lamusalatina.com

Museo Chicote

As you'll see from the paparazzi shots of Dalí, Lorca, Buñuel and Almodóvar, this bar on Gran Vía has been a favourite haunt of all the movers and shakers of Madrid since the 1930s. It's still the main stomping ground for both the city's trendy set and their arch rivals, the posh *pijos*, and is a perfect place to start or end an evening. Legend has it that the bar was once staffed by hookers who would be picked out by the punters and, after their shift, would scuttle down a secret passage to (no sniggering at the back, please) Bar Cock (T 91 532 2826) on the neighbouring street for a rendezvous.

Calle Gran Vía 12, T 91 532 6737, www.museo-chicote.com

La Terraza del Casino

If you've never had the chance to sample the legendary Ferran Adrià's amazing culinary alchemy at El Bulli (T 97 215 0457), this place runs it a close second. Its acclaimed chef, Paco Roncero, cut his teeth as one of Adrià's disciples and still spends time at his mentor's food lab in Barcelona, as well as running El Bulli Catering in Madrid. Despite the extraordinary experimental menu here,

La Terraza's vibe is distinctly traditional: the classical interiors reflect the former opulence of the Casino de Madrid and the dress code is strictly jacket and a tie for gentlemen. The central location on Calle de Alcalá gives the summer terrace the added grandeur of unrivalled views of the city.
Calle de Alcalá 15, T 91 532 1275, www.casinodemadrid.com

Club 31

A favourite with Madrid's high society set since the 1950s, this little gem has recently been refurbished with white ostrich-skin walls, groovy lamps and Starck Louis Ghost chairs. The cocktail bar hasn't lost any of its class and the menu hasn't changed much either – it still serves retro classics such as foie gras lasagne, crêpe Suzette and potato soufflé, although Ángel Paracuellos, the chef for over a quarter of a century, has added more modern dishes like tuna tartar with wasabi sauce. The service is razor-sharp thanks to the attention of executive manager Miguel Ángel García, who also runs some of Madrid's other top-drawer eateries including the chic and labyrinthine Chinese Le Dragón (T 91 435 6668) and the East Asian and Vietnamese Café Saigon (T 91 563 1566). *Calle de Alcalá 58, T 91 531 0092, www.club31.net*

Citra

After taking a leisurely turn around design emporium Vinçon in swanky Salamanca district, pop next door to Citra to sample the modern Mediterranean fare with Asian accents of young Venezuelan chef Elías Murciano, who trained under top-drawer culinary titans including Alain Ducasse. Although the menu is dictated by seasonal ingredients, seven of the dishes are always on offer thanks to the demands of its regular clients. Plump for the terrine of foie gras and carpaccio of figs with Campari jelly and finish with chocolate soufflé with pineapple foam and raspberry ice cream. Or if you're merely peckish, settle down in the casual dining corner and grab a drink and a round of *pinchos* (tapas). *Calle de Castelló 18, T 91 575 2866*

Bar del Diego

The discreet, sliding glass doors of this tiny drinking den, tucked away on a street that runs parallel to Gran Vía, lead to a small bar that at first glance can seem rather disappointing thanks to its pared-down décor. Bar del Diego isn't a showy establishment, though – it's all about intimacy and excellent cocktails, which the dishy black-tie-clad staff fix up in a flash. Arrive at around 8pm to grab one of the few tables for a couple of rounds of pre-prandial mojitos or martinis, or pop in after dinner before stumbling on to Bar Cock (T 91 532 2826) a couple of doors up, or Museo Chicote (see p056).
Calle de la Reina 12, T 91 523 3106

El Chaflán

Chef Juan Pablo Felipe has earned a Michelin star by creating modern, avant-garde Mediterranean dishes using fresh Spanish produce with a nod to traditional local cuisine. Meals at his chic, open-plan joint kick off with amazing deconstructed cocktails and finish with a real flourish of modern petit fours. In between, order the mushroom risotto or tuna from southern Spain, which are both among the specialities. Lunch is a particularly pleasant affair and easily worth the taxi ride out of the city centre. The simply decorated space, dominated by a large potted olive tree, is floodlit by the skylight and the only distraction from the food, the genteel setting and the slick service is the frenetic activity in the glassed-off kitchen. *Avenida de Pío XII 34, T 91 350 6193, www.elchaflan.com*

Janatomo

One of Madrid's most celebrated Asian eateries has moved from its original location to a new space on the same street in Chueca. It still serves up high-quality, well-priced sushi, noodles and other oriental specialities, but the interiors have been changed to a sort of modern zen. The designer chairs, including Vitra's reissue of the legendary Eames 'Fibreglass Chair', wooden floors,

metal and glass are reminiscent of Barcelona's style-obsessed, fashionable restaurants, but the space is at once contemporary and cosy. If you're feeling adventurous, ask to sit at one of the *yakiniku* tables on which you can cook your own food.
Calle de la Reina 27, T 91 521 5566

Ølsen

One of the trendiest eateries in the city serves up not Spanish but Scandinavian food. Following hot on the heels of the first, spectacularly successful Ølsen (T 00 54 4776 7677), which opened in Buenos Aires' trendy Palermo Viejo neighbourhood, this second venture also has a menu offering a mélange of Northern European dishes, including salmon, blinis, reindeer steaks, mussels and berries. Soft yellow lighting and wood furnishings make for a welcoming space packed with the city's beau monde, who prop up the cocktail bar (the only one in Madrid to serve spiced and fruit-flavoured vodkas) and lounge about in the chill-out area being serenaded by local DJs until the small hours in true Madrileño fashion. *Calle del Prado 15, T 91 429 3659, www.olsenmadrid.com*

Nodo

This is one of the few restaurants that enjoyed the boom of fusion cuisine during the 1990s and survived the backlash when it fell out of fashion. The menu still works well, taking a Mediterranean approach to Japanese food, but the clientele has changed from cool to distinctly corporate. Although the staff tend to be uppity and unwelcoming, the sleek, minimal interiors and elegant zen garden have aged well and retained an intimacy that have earned Nodo the accolade of being one of the city's contemporary classic eateries. Ask for a table next to the kitchen window to watch the chefs at work.
Calle de Velázquez 150, T 91 564 4044

Suite Café Club

The success of this place is not down to its rather average Mediterranean menu but its industrial interiors, retro furnishings and spacious summer terrace planted with cypress trees, which is always packed with Madrid's beau monde before they head off to the clubs. Rock up for an early drink at around 10.30pm before the space gets inundated after 1.30am with equal numbers of gay and straight party people.

Then embark on a bar crawl starting at the lounge bar at Hotel de Las Letras (see p033), moving on to Museo Chicote (see p056), Bar del Diego (see p061) or Bar Cock (T 91 532 2826) before following the fashionistas to The Room (T 91 523 8654) for retro techno with a touch of glamour. *Calle de la Virgen de los Peligros 4, T 91 521 4031, www.suitecafeclub.com*

Mood
Upscale convenience store-cum-diner
chain VIPS has been a part of Madrid's
restaurant scene since the 1970s and
is now behind a new chain of cafés that
combine quality food at rock-bottom
prices with high-end design. Head to
Mood in Majadahonda where you can
dine in elegant surroundings for €15.
Avenida de los Reyes Católicos 6,
T 91 275 0542

INSIDER'S GUIDE

ALMUDENA BUSTOS, ARCHITECT

Our muse in Madrid, Almudena Bustos, works at Estudio Lamela, the high-profile architects' practice most renowned for creating the new Terminal Four at Barajas Airport in partnership with Richard Rogers. When she's not up to her eyeballs in CADs or choosing fonts for re-branding projects, she can be found kicking up her heels in hotspots around Chueca and La Latina.

Her favourites include Bazaar (Calle de la Libertad 21, T 91 523 3905) for its great design and fantastic food that never exceeds €8 a dish, Café Oliver (Calle de Almirante 12, T 91 521 7379) for brunch or drinks and good music, and Café Belén (Calle Belén 5, T 91 308 2747) for its authentic, laid-back atmosphere, good coffee and extensive menu of cocktails and teas. In summer she loves La Latina's buzzy Plaza de la Paja and recommends coffee or cocktails at Delic (Costanilla de San Andrés 14, T 91 364 5450) and lunch or dinner at El Almendro (Calle de Almendro 13, T 91 523 8654). Ene (Calle del Nuncio 19, T 91 366 2591) is best for brunch, while a drink on the terrace of El Viajero (Plaza de la Cebada 11, T 91 366 9064) is a must after a browse in El Rastro market.

In central Madrid, her two favourite haunts are Scandinavian joint Ølsen (see p064) and bar and restaurant Jazzanova (Paseo de la Castellana 8, T 91 578 3487). And at the end of the night, the chicest places to shake a leg is the former concert hall El Sol (Calle de Jardines 3, T 91 532 6490).

ARCHITOUR

A GUIDE TO MADRID'S ICONIC BUILDINGS

Everything about Madrid has the elegant assurance of a great capital. Grand boulevards converge at neo-classical fountains; winged lions atop José Rafael Moneo's magnificently renovated Estación de Atocha (see p079) eyeball the frolicking Greek gods on Ricardo Velázquez Bosco's improbably opulent agriculture ministry; and Paseo del Prado, the promenade between the main museums, is sheltered by sycamores and white magnolia trees.

However, when it comes to modern architecture, there is nothing that comes close to the in-your-face coups of other Spanish cities, like Gehry's Guggenheim in Bilbao, save perhaps Barajas Airport (opposite). For one thing there isn't enough space in the city's jam-packed ancient centre. For another, General Franco wasn't exactly an archi buff. When Luis Buñuel came to Madrid to shoot *Viridiana* in 1960, he rented an apartment in what he reckoned was the only skyscraper. There are lots more now – notably Torres Blancas (see p076) – but Madrid is still stronger at restoring old treasures than building new ones. There's the 18th-century hospital that's now the Museo Nacional Reina Sofía (see p045) and the Villahermosa Palace, which Rafael Moneo turned into a home for the Museo Thyssen-Bornemisza (see p042). His extension to the Museo Nacional del Prado (Paseo del Prado, T 91 330 2800) opens in 2007.

For all addresses, see Resources.

Barajas Airport

Richard Rogers' stunning airport building has a good claim to be the best-looking in the world. The undulating bamboo awnings of his new Terminal Four guide passengers subliminally through check-in and boarding with a clever colour-coding system and a series of beautiful skylights that illuminate the space with Spanish sunshine. And it's not all about aesthetics, either. Just as impressive is the automatic luggage-sorting system, SATE, which uses no manpower and distributes all the bags to the planes automatically from a bomb-proof bunker. It's just a shame that the plaudits have to stop there. Because the management is shambolic and staff still don't seem to know where anything is.
T 91 305 8345, www.aena.es

Terminal Four, Barajas Airport

Torres Blancas

Local architect Francisco Javier Sáenz de Oíza made his name in the city with a series of sober Meisian row houses in Entrevías in the 1950s. By 1968, when he built Torres Blancas, he had become a whole lot more daring. This apartment block may no longer have the brilliant white colour that gave it its name but it's still the most desirable address in the city for local architects and design aficionados. The public has to make do with admiring its bulbous columns from the Avenida de América, but an invitation inside will reveal internal doors of rose-coloured glass and a round lift, which is mimicked by a series of circular terraces.
Avenida de América 37

Faro de la Moncloa

Another beneficiary of the building blitz of 1992, when Barcelona hosted the summer Olympics from a rebuilt city, Seville was the venue for the World Expo and Madrid, eager not to be left behind, was named the European City of Culture. Architect of the tower Salvador Pérez Arroyo, together with his partner Eva Hurtado, haven't had the same degree of popular success as many of the others who contributed projects in that same miraculous year, but were astonishingly influential among their peers, not least in their use of computers to help with the design process. The tower, standing 92m high, still looks impossibly modern today and offers a great view back over the city. *Avenida del Arco de la Victoria, T 91 544 8104*

Catalana Occidente

Floating gracefully at the end of the Paseo de la Castellana, this elegant cantilevered office block built by Rafael de La-Hoz has an outer skin of tempered structural glazing, giving it a ghostly glow at night. Even the entrance, with a long staircase leading up a grassy embankment, has a certain retro glamour to it. Rafael de La-Hoz was originally a Cordoba-based firm, founded as far back as 1919 but has emerged as one of the more inventive local practices, working wonders with small budgets on jobs that the starrier names might well find beneath them. *Paseo de la Castellana 50, www.rafaeldelahoz.com*

Estación de Atocha

Internationally known for the tragic 2004 bombings, this station complex is perfect for a cultural comedown after visiting the Museo Nacional Reina Sofía (see p045). Either chill out or warm up in the palm-filled, temperature-controlled garden that was designed by Rafael Moneo. Atocha has always had a fabulous architectural pedigree – among the architects to work on the rebuilt 1892 building was Gustave

Eiffel. Moneo added a 1992 extension that quadrupled the capacity – the old station has been turned into a concourse of shops and cafés (above). The slender columns of the new building are the most immediately impressive feature but do not miss the parking area outside where the canopies make a dramatic statement from Spain's pre-eminently understated architect.
Glorieta Carlos V, T 90 224 3402

SHOPPING

THE CITY'S BEST SHOPS AND WHAT TO BUY

The Colette-style concept store has hit Madrid in a big way, with Gallery (see p197), Isolée (see p195) and Maison Blanche (see p193) offering a one-stop shopping experience, from clothes to food to music. If you plan to spend your Euros on local fashion labels and have limited time, stick to certain areas of the city. The streets between Calle Conde Duque and Plaza Comendadoras have the best menswear outlets, including Sportivo (Calle de Conde Duque 31, T :2 653 6772) for chic streetwear , Mini (Calle Cristo 8, T :2 659 1946), which is stuffed with smart suits, and Duke (Calle de Conde Duque 39, T :2 653 595:) for shoes.

Chic cul-de-sac Callejón de Jorge Juan in Salamanca is a haven for local couture and prêt-à-porter for the ladies. At number 25 is Scooter (T :2 687 585:), a favourite with the city's fashionistas, while number 23 is the eponymous outlet of Sybilla Sorondo (T :2 689 2433), who has been designing frocks, textiles, accessories and even homewares for the avant-garde end of Spanish society for 31 years. Her diffusion range for teens is called Jocomomola , a pun on Madrileño slang which roughly translates as 'Wow, how cool is that!' Another unmissable outlet for the globetrotting girl-about-town is the refurbished Mott (Barquillo 42, T :2 419 2391), a real Aladdin's Cave of accessories hand-picked from around the world by super-cool proprietress Laura Losada.

For all addresses, see Resources.

Vinçon

The capital's premier design emporium is housed in an old red-brick factory set around a spacious patio. It stocks all the usual classics plus some great Spanish products like these placemats depicting the city's architectural icons (€6.90 for the set). If you're after some bespoke illumination for your pad, take a left as you enter to find an enormous lighting section. Knick-knacks, children's toys and office gadgetry are also on the ground floor. For bathroom fixtures and accessories, crockery, cutlery, books or kitchen gadgets, stick to the first floor. *Calle de Castelló 18, T 91 578 0520, www.vincon.com*

Maison Blanche

This achingly fashionable, Philippe Starck-style, white-on-white concept store is a haven for foodies. The deli supermarket sells upmarket foodstuffs from around the world and the global theme is continued in the restaurant where the menu offers up traditional national dishes. But the real draw is the winery, which stocks a selection of fashionable Spanish vintages. The in-house sommelier has eschewed the usual flowery winespeak when it comes to picking out his favourites from the cellar and has come up with quirky suggestions for the best bottle of vino for your father, your mother, an evening with friends, or even a night of passion.
Calle del Piamonte 10, T 91 522 8217

Isolée

If Wallpaper* decided to storm the retail sector, it might look like this. Located just a couple of blocks from Gran Vía, Isolée is a treasure trove of clothes, accessories, food and homewares, all hand-picked to appeal to the style-conscious jetsetter. There is a fine selection of the best pieces from international fashion labels, including PLAY by Comme des Garçons, RED Valentino and Duffer of St George, plus a host of the best Spanish designer pieces by Mónica García, Juan Antonio López, Mireya Ruiz and our current favourite purveyor of funky frocks, Ailanto. After splashing out on a new wardrobe, download the latest dance classics onto your iPod and pop downstairs to the bar for a drink to recover from retail overload. *Calle de las Infantas 19, T 91 524 1298, www.isolee.com*

Hespen & Suárez

When American entrepreneur Kay Hespen and her Spanish husband José Suárez's catering business started to become hugely successful, they branched out into retail. Their first outlet, which has a logo and layout similar to New York's legendary upmarket grocery chain Dean & Deluca (T 00 1 212 226 6800), started off stocking crockery, cut flowers, foodstuffs, cookbooks, fresh bread and a range of 18 takeaway dishes a day. Now the couple have their own range of wines, cookies, jam and bars of the traditional Spanish nougat Turrón, €5.25 (above). In March 2006, they opened a second branch, a third followed in the summer, and they plan to have 40 shops by 2010. Watch that diet go out the window.
Calle Barceló 15, T 91 445 3903,
www.hespenysuarez.com

Gallery

Although chic Callejón de Jorge Juan is principally a happy hunting ground for female fashionistas, this street also has a haven for the male of the species in Gallery. Premier interior designer Tomás Alía has created a huge new space (the shop was previously a few doors down) for an impressive collection of shoes, bags, belts, CDs, smart suits and casualwear. Designer shaving sets, aftershaves and a great range of beautifully packaged toiletries make Gallery the perfect pit stop for the well-groomed metrosexual and there's even a mineral water bar to avoid the terrible sin of dehydration. *Calle de Jorge Juan 38, T 91 576 7931, www.gallerymadrid.com*

Marre Moerel Design Studio

Acclaimed Dutch designer Marre Moerel's beautiful, organic and quirky ceramic lighting and tableware has been snapped up by interiors firm Cappellini (which bought two collections), and exhibited at design fairs and in museums across the globe. Get your hands on both limited-edition pieces and prototypes, such as her bulbous 'Barnacle Tiles' towel hooks and caterpillar-like 'Polyp Light', €220 (above), which can be bought at her tiny shop. Moerel will happily ship your purchase in an enormous pass-the-parcel-style box of bubble wrap. *Calle de Noviciado 4, T 91 523 9059, www.marremoerel.com*

SPORTS AND SPAS

WORK OUT, CHILL OUT OR JUST WATCH

The fact that two of the most popular newspapers in Spain, *La Marca* and *AS*, are mainly devoted to football gives an indication as to the extent of the national obsession with the beautiful game. And even if you're not that into the sport, watching the Galáticos play for Real Madrid at the Estadio Santiago Bernabéu (see p092), a magnificent steep-tiered concrete bowl, is an uplifting and quintessentially Madrileño experience. But the Spaniards are also aficionados of a whole host of other sports apart from football, with basketball coming in as a close second. The city's two main teams, Adecco Estudiantes and Real Madrid, can both be seen at the Palacio Vistalegre (Calle Serrano 95, T 91 563 9493). And if you're not averse to a controversial display of animal cruelty, then see a bullfight at the Plaza de Toros de las Ventas (Calle Alcalá 237, T 91 356 2200).

For a more gentle and participatory form of exercise, book a walking tour through the mountains with Haciendo Huella (José Abascal 24, T 91 593 0441) or a more adrenalin-fuelled adventure with Arawak Viajes (Calle de las Peñuelas 15, T 91 474 2524). Bravo Bike (Calle de la Montera 25-27, T 91 559 5523) offers guided bicycle tours around the city or further afield. Golf fans should head for the Olivar de La Hinojosa Golf Club (Avenida Dublin, T 91 721 1889) which has 18 holes, tennis courts and a pool.

For all addresses, see Resources.

Maravillas Gymnasium

This mostly wooden gym attached to a high school is more suited to the architecture buff with a passing interest in working up a sweat than to the dedicated fitness fanatic, as the facilities have changed little since it was built by acclaimed Spanish architect Alejandro de la Sota in 1961. Classrooms are cleverly folded over the athletics track in search of the sunlight, which gives the old wooden interiors a golden glow and the rooms are functional but designed with great finesse. This modernist icon was the only building that Mies van der Rohe insisted on seeing on his last trip to Spain so if you only go to gawp don't feel guilty as it's certain that he never went near the changing rooms. *Calle Joaquín Costa 21-23, T 91 564 6598*

Metropolitan Gym and Spa

Spain's Metropolitan gyms have dispelled the drudgery of keeping in shape through elegant, ethereal design accompanied by spa facilities and beauty therapies to die for. There are fitness classes every day (8am-10pm on weekdays; 10am-8pm at weekends) including Pilates, aerobics and spinning, plus a host of off-beat circuit training sessions, from hardcore Body Hunting to Asian-inspired Cardio-Box and Chi-Kung. In the 'water zone' (right), bathers float above jets from stainless-steel 'water beds', before heading off to the Turkish bath. If you're not in the mood to work up a sweat, head for the 500 sq m Balneario for a manicure, pedicure, facial or Shiatsu massage and afterwards nibble daintily on something healthy in the café-restaurant with immaculately groomed Madrileños.
Calle José Abascal 46, T 91 451 4466,
www.clubmetropolitan.net

Please delete address not required before mailing

PHAIDON PRESS LIMITED

Regent's Wharf

All Saints Street

London N1 9PA

PHAIDON PRESS INC.

180 Varick Street

New York

NY 10014

Return address for USA and Canada only

*Return address for UK and countries
outside the USA and Canada only*

Dear Reader, Books by Phaidon are recognised world-wide for their beauty, scholarship and elegance.
We invite you to return this card with your name and e-mail address so that we can keep you informed
of our new publications, special offers and events. Alternatively, visit us at **www.phaidon.com** to
see our entire list of books, videos and stationery. Register on-line to be included on our regular e-newsletters.

Subjects in which I have a special interest

☐ General Non-Fiction   ☐ Art   ☐ Photography   ☐ Architecture   ☐ Design

☐ Fashion   ☐ Music   ☐ Children's   ☐ Food   ☐ Travel

	Mr/Miss/Ms	Initial	Surname
Name			
No./Street			
City			
Post code/Zip code		Country	
E-mail			

This is not an order form. To order please contact Customer Services at the appropriate address overleaf.

Estadio Santiago Bernabéu
After a makeover by Lamela Architects, Real Madrid's home has now achieved five-star status with enough high-tech facilities for even the most highly paid footballer. If your trip doesn't coincide with a home match, you can still book a tour around the pitch, the dressing rooms and the trophies exhibition. *Avenida de Concha Espina 1, T 91 398 4300, www.realmadrid.es*

The Lab Room
The Occidental Miguel Angel hotel may
be five star but it's unremarkable apart
from its two Michelin-starred restaurant
La Broche and fab 700 sq m spa. The
day rate of €40 gets you access to the
pool, gym (staffed by physiotherapists)
and indulgent Jacuzzis – massages,
manicures and pedicures are extra.
Calle Miguel Angel 31, T 91 442 0022,
www.occidentalhotels.com

ESCAPES

WHERE TO GO IF YOU WANT TO LEAVE TOWN

Bang in the centre of Spain, Madrid is the hub of the transport network, so fleeing the capital for a change of pace, a couple of days on the coast or an insight into the defiantly different regions is simple. There are several shuttle flights an hour to Barcelona as well as the supersonic 300km per hour AVE train which was introduced as a fast link to Seville for the Expo there in 1992.

Meanwhile, day trips can provide a rich backdrop to the history and culture of the capital. Felipe II's vast palace-monastery El Escorial (www.patrimonio.nacional.es), 45km north-west of the capital, has little of the grace and majesty of similar mono-maniacal building projects such as Louis XIV's Château de Versailles (www.chateauversailles.fr), but it beats them hands-down when it comes to artwork. The Bourbon apartments are adorned with beautiful tapestries from cartoons by Goya, the Museo de Pintura has works by Titian, El Greco, Rubens and Ribera and the Salas Capitulares is stuffed with yet more treasures displayed beneath delicately painted 16th-century ceilings. Nearby, a massive cross (allegedly the tallest in the world) heralds the tomb of Spain's despot from the recent past – Franco's El Valle de Los Caídos (www. patrimonio.nacional.es). Many Republican prisoners of war died constructing this vast, brutalist basilica built into the mountain, meant to commemorate the Civil War dead of both sides.

For all addresses, see Resources.

Toledo

If El Greco's haunting portraits and the languid figures depicted in his religious paintings caught your eye in the Museo Nacional del Prado (T 91 330 2800), head for the beguiling city of Toledo to ogle more of his masterpieces. The cathedral houses his magnificent *Expolio de Cristo* depicting the disrobing of Christ as well as works by Velázquez, Rubens, Titian, Raphael and Caravaggio. But yet more spectacular is *The Burial of the Count of Orgaz* in the Iglesia de Santo Tomé, which is a sort of 16th-century *Hello!*-style who's who, with the heavenly host regally presiding over an impossibly glamorous wake. Take the 6.50am AVE train from Estación de Atocha (see p079) and visit in the low season to avoid the tourist hordes. *Puerta de Bisagra, Toledo, T 92 522 0843, www.castillalamancha.es*

MUSAC
León's Museo de Arte Contemporáneo de
Castilla y León has been acquiring
cutting-edge, contemporary art from
around the world since 2003. The 900
works displayed in the warren of square
and rhomboid buildings designed by
architects Mansilla and Tuñón
constitutes the first of five phases.
*Avenida de los Reyes Leoneses 24, León,
T 98 709 0000, www.musac.org.es*

Jardín de la Isla, Aranjuez
In the 17th and 18th centuries, Madrid's
royal court spurned the green spaces of
the Retiro in the spring and autumn in
favour of the 300 acres of magnificent
gardens at Aranjuez that surround the
lavish Royal Palace built there by the
Bourbons. If you plan to frolic amid the
fountains and picnic beside the Parterre,
pick a weekend between late April and
July or from mid-September until mid-
October to catch an original 19th-century
steam train to Aranjuez called the Tren de
la Fresa, which is staffed by stewardesses
in period dress serving platters of plump,
fresh strawberries for which the area is
renowned. Also worth a visit is the Royal
Palace itself, which dates from the reign
of Philip II and is famous for its 'Hall of
Mirrors' and a spectacular collection of
Spanish porcelain.
Plaza de Parejas, Aranjuez, T 91 891 1344,
www.patrimonionacional.es

Segovia

A stunning city hewn from golden stone, Segovia's architecture is a potted history of Iberia. Gawp at the Roman aqueduct that soars 28.1m above Plaza Azoguejo, marvel at the 16th-century gothic cathedral (pictured) in Plaza Major and take a trip to Alcázar Castle, with its fairy-tale turrets and spires.
Tourist information: Plaza Major 10, Segovia, T 92 146 0334

NOTES

SKETCHES AND MEMOS

RESOURCES
ADDRESSES AND ROOM RATES

LANDMARKS
009 Caixa Forum Madrid
Calles de Alameda and Almadén
www.fundacio.lacaixa.es

009 El Matadero
Paseo de la Chopera 12
T 91 480 4968
www.mataderomadrid.com

009 Palacio Real
Calle Bailén
T 91 454 8800
www.patrimonio nacional.es

009 Torres KIO
Plaza Castilla

010 Palacio de Congresos
Paseo de la Castellana 99
T 91 337 8100
www.madridconvention centre.com

010 Open Air Sculpture Museum
Paseo de la Castellana 41
T 91 701 1863

012 Torre Picasso
Plaza de Pablo Ruíz Picasso

013 Teatro Valle-Inclán
Plaza Lavapiés
T 91 505 8800

014 Centro Colón
Plaza de Colón

014 Museo Arqueológico Nacional
Calle de Serrano 13
T 91 577 7912

015 Círculo de Bellas Artes
Calle de Alcalá 42
T 91 360 5400
www.circulobellas artes.com

HOTELS
016 Hotel Ritz
Room rates:
double, €480
Plaza de la Lealtad 5
T 91 701 6767
www.ritzmadrid.com

016 Hard Rock Hotel
Room rates:
double, €235
Plaza de Santa Ana 14
T 91 531 4500
www.hardrockhotel madrid.com

016 Hotel Villa Magna
Room rates:
double, €275
Paseo de la Castellana 22
T 91 587 1234
www.madrid.hyatt.com

016 The Westin Palace Hotel
Room rates:
double, €239
Plaza de las Cortes 7
T 91 360 8000
www.westinpalace madrid.com

017 Mario
Room rates:
double, €90;
Junior Suite, €115
Calle de Campomanes 4
T 91 548 8548
www.room-mate hoteles.com

020 Hotel Quo
Room rates:
double, €225;
Junior Suite, €250;
Superior Room 702, €200
Calle de Sevilla 4
T 91 532 9049
www.hotelesquo.com

022 Vincci Soho
Room rates:
double, €146;
Standard Room, €146
Calle de Prado 18
T 91 141 4100
www.vinccihoteles.com

022 Vincci Centrum
Room rates:
double, €116
Calle Cedaceros 4
T 91 360 4720
www.vinccihoteles.com

024 Urban
Room rates:
double, €257;
Royal Suite, €1000
Carrera de San Jerónimo 34
T 91 787 7770
www.derbyhotels.es

026 Palacio del Retiro
Room rates:
double, €315;
Luxury Suite,
€381-€855
Calle de Alfonso XII 14
T 91 523 7460
www.ac-hotels.com
028 Hotel Puerta
América
Room rates:
double, €190;
First Floor Room, €360
Avenida de América 41
T 91 744 5400
www.hotel
puertamerica.com
032 Alicia
Room rates:
double, €100;
Duplexes 401
and 501, €215
Calle del Prado 2
T 91 389 6095
www.room-mate
hoteles.com
033 Hotel de las Letras
Room rates:
double, €140;
Standard Double
Room, €140;
Plus Room, €175
Calle Gran Vía 11
T 91 523 7980
www.hoteldelasletras.com
033 Bauza
Room rates:
double, €158
Calle de Goya 79
T 91 435 7545

036 Santo Mauro
Room rates:
double, €315
Calle de Zurbano 36
T 91 319 6900
www.ac-hotels.com
038 Hotel Meninas
Room rates:
double, €93-€185;
Junior Suite, €120-€240;
Suites Especial, €235-€260
Calle de Campomanes 7
T 91 541 2805
www.hotelmeninas.com
038 Posada del Peine
Room rates:
double, €90
Calle de Postas 17
T 91 523 8151
www.hthoteles.com

24 HOURS
040 Centro Conde Duque
Calle de Conde Duque 9-11
T 91 588 5861
www.munimadrid.es
040 Museo de Escultura
al Aire Libre
Paseo de la Castellana 41
T 91 701 1863
www.munimadrid.es
040 Museo Nacional
del Prado
Paseo del Prado
T 91 330 2800
www.museoprado.es
040 Museo Sorolla
General Martínez Campos 37
T 91 310 1584
http://museo
sorolla.mcu.es

040 Residencia
de Estudiantes
Calle de Pinar 21-23
T 91 563 6411
www.residencia.csic.es
041 Cacao Sampaka
Calle de Orellana 4
T 91 319 5840
www.cacaosampaka.com
042 Museo Thyssen-
Bornemisza
Paseo del Prado 8
T 91 369 0151
www.museothyssen.org
044 Arola
Calle de Argumosa 43
T 91 467 0202
www.arola-madrid.com
044 La Broche
Calle Miguel Angel 29
T 91 399 3437
www.labroche.com
044 Hotel Arts
Carrer de la Marina 19-21
Barcelona
T 93 483 8065
www.ritzcarlton.com/
hotels/barcelona
045 Museo Nacional
Reina Sofía
Calle Santa Isabel 52
T 91 774 1000
www.museoreinasofia.es
046 Nueva Fontana
Calle de Hernani 75
T 91 417 5693
www.lanuevafontana.com
046 Le Ki
Calle de la Paz 5

046 Franela Dance Hall
Calle Mesonero
Romanos 13
T 91 541 3500
www.tripfamily.com

URBAN LIFE
048 Asador
Donostiarra
Calle Infanta Mercedes 79
T 91 579 6264
048 La Dorada
Calle de Orense 64
T 91 570 2004
048 Lhardy
Carrera San Jerónimo 8
T 91 522 0731
048 Teatriz
Calle Hermosilla 15
T 91 577 5379
048 Viuda de Vacas
Calle Cava Alta 23
T 91 366 5847
049 Sopa
Calle de Nieremberg 23
T 91 413 1719
www.sopa.vg
050 Fast Good
Calle de Padre Damián 23
T 91 343 0655
www.fast-good.com
050 El Bulli
Cala Montjoi
Roses (Girona)
T 97 215 0457
www.elbulli.com

052 Wagaboo
Calle de Gravina 18
T 91 531 6567
www.wagaboo.com
052 Le Dragón
Gil de Santibáñez 6
T 91 435 6668
053 Bajó Cero
Glorieta de Quevedo 6
T 91 445 3827
www.bajocero.es
053 Giangrossi
Calle de Alberto Aguilera 1
T 91 444 0130
www.giangrossi.es
054 Ojalá
Calle San Andrés 1
T 91 523 2747
www.lamusalatina.com
054 La Musa Latina
Calle San Andrés 1
T 91 354 0255
www.lamusalatina.com
056 Museo Chicote
Calle Gran Vía 12
T 91 532 6737
www.museo-chicote.com
056 Bar Cock
Calle de la Reina 16
T 91 532 2826
057 La Terraza
del Casino
Calle de Alcalá 15
T 91 532 1275
www.casinode
madrid.com
058 Club 31
Calle de Alcalá 58
T 91 531 0092
www.club31.net

058 Café Saigon
Paseo de la Castellana 66
T 91 563 1566
060 Citra
Calle de Castelló 18
T 91 575 2866
061 Bar del Diego
Calle de la Reina 12
T 91 523 3106
062 El Chaflán
Avenida de Pío XII 34
T 91 350 6193
www.elchaflan.com
063 Janatomo
Calle de la Reina 27
T 91 521 5566
064 Ølsen
Calle del Prado 15
T 91 429 3659
www.olsenmadrid.com
064 Ølsen
Gorriti 5870
Palermo
Buenos Aires
Argentina
T 00 54 4776 7677
066 Nodo
Calle de Velázquez 150
T 91 564 4044
067 Suite Café Club
Calle de la Virgen de los
Peligros 4
T 91 521 4031
www.suitecafeclub.com
067 The Room
Arlabán 7
T 91 523 8654
www.theroomclub.com

068 Mood
Avenida de los Reyes
Católicos 6
T 91 275 0542

070 Bazaar
Calle de la Libertad 21
T 91 523 3905

070 Café Belén
Calle Belén 5
T 91 308 2747

070 Café Oliver
Calle Almirante 12
T 91 521 7379

070 Delic
Costanilla de San
Andrés 14
T 91 364 5450

070 El Almendro
Calle Almendro 13
T 91 365 4252

070 Ene
Calle del Nuncio 19
T 91 366 2591
www.enerestaurante.com

070 Jazzanova
Paseo de la Castellana 8
T 91 578 3487

070 El Sol
Calle de Jardines 3
T 91 532 6490

070 El Viajero
Plaza de la Cebada 11
T 91 366 9064

ARCHITOUR
073 Barajas Airport
T 91 305 8345
www.aena.es
076 Torres Blancas
Avenida de América 37

077 Faro de la Moncloa
Avenida del Arco
de la Victoria
T 91 544 8104

078 Catalana
Occidente
Paseo de la Castellana 50
www.rafaeldelahoz.com

079 Estacíon de Atocha
Glorieta Carlos V
T 90 224 3402

SHOPPING
080 Duke
Calle Conde de Duque 28
T 91 542 4849

080 Mini
Calle Cristo 7
T 91 548 0835

080 Mott
Barquillo 31
T 91 308 1280

080 Scooter
Callejón de Jorge Juan 14
T 91 576 4749

080 Sportivo
Calle de Conde Duque 28
T 91 542 5661

080 Sybilla Sorondo
Callejón de Jorge Juan 12
T 91 578 1322
www.sybilla.es

081 Vinçon
Calle de Castelló 18
T 91 578 0520
www.vincon.com

082 Maison Blanche
Calle del Piamonte 10
T 91 522 8217

084 Isolée
Calle de las Infantas 19
T 91 524 1298
www.isolee.com

085 Hespen y Suárez
Calle Barceló 15
T 91 445 3903
Calle Principe de
Vergara 93
T 91 564 9024
Calle de Orense 22
www.hespenysuarez.com

085 Dean & Deluca
560 Broadway
New York, USA
T 00 1 212 226 6800

086 Gallery
Calle de Jorge Juan 38
T 91 576 7931
www.gallerymadrid.com

087 Marre Moerel
Design Studio
Calle de Noviciado 4
T 91 523 9059
www.marremoerel.com

SPORTS AND SPAS
088 Arawak Viajes
Calle de las Peñuelas 15
T 91 474 2524
www.arawakviajes.com

088 Bravo Bike
Calle de la Montera 25-27
T 91 559 5523
www.bravobike.com

WALLPAPER* CITY GUIDES

Editorial Director
Richard Cook

Art Director
Loran Stosskopf
City Editor
Alvaro Castro
Series Editor
Jeroen Bergmans
Project Editor
Rachael Moloney
**Executive
Managing Editor**
Jessica Firmin

Chief Designer
Ben Blossom
Designers
Sara Martin
Ingvild Sandal
Map Illustrator
Russell Bell

Photography Editor
Alicia Foley
Photography Assistant
Jasmine Labeau

Chief Sub-Editor
Jeremy Case
Sub-Editor
Clive Morris
Editorial Assistant
Felicity Cloake

**Wallpaper* Group
Editor-in-Chief**
Jeremy Langmead
Creative Director
Tony Chambers
Publishing Director
Fiona Dent

Thanks to
Paul Barnes
Emma Blau
David McKendrick
Claudia Perin
Meirion Pritchard

PHAIDON

Phaidon Press Limited
Regent's Wharf
All Saints Street
London N1 9PA

Phaidon Press Inc
180 Varick Street
New York, NY 10014

www.phaidon.com

First published 2006
© 2006 Phaidon Press
Limited

ISBN 0 7148 4684 8

A CIP Catalogue record for
this book is available from
the British Library.

All prices are correct at
time of going to press, but
are subject to change.

Printed in China

PHOTOGRAPHERS

Gregori Civera
Palacio de Congresos,
pp010-011
Centro Colón, p014
Círculo de Bellas Artes,
p015
Mario, p017, pp018-019
Hotel Meninas, pp038-039
Ojalá, pp054-055
El Chaflán, p062
Janatomo, p063
Nodo, p066
Suite Café Club, p067

Roger Davies
City view, inside cover
Hotel Quo, p020, p021
Museo Chicote, p056
Club 31, pp058-059
Bar del Diego, p061
Almudena Bustos, p071
Torres Blancas, p076
Faro de la Moncloa, p077
Catalana Occidente, p078
Estación de Atocha, p079
Estadio Santiago
Bernabéu, pp092-093

Pedro D'Orey
Isolée, p084

Amparo Garrido
Barajas Airport,
pp074-075

Katsuhisa Kida
Barajas Airport, p073

Angel Marcos
MUSAC, pp098-099

Philippe Ruault
Museo Nacional Reina
Sofía, p045

Eva Serrats
Museo Thyssen-
Bornemisza, p042, p043

Jason Tozer
Vinçon, p081
Hespen & Suárez, p085
Marre Moerel Design
Studio, p087

Turespaña
Jardín de la Isla, Aranjuez,
pp100-101
Segovia, pp100-101

MADRID

A COLOUR-CODED GUIDE TO THE CITY'S HOT 'HOODS

SALAMANCA
Playground of the upper classes and media types, and the luxury shops they covet

CASTELLANA
The city's main artery flanked by office skyscrapers and hidden cultural gems

CHUECA
Want a night on the town? Head to this lively area for funky bars and cheap eats

MALASAÑA
Birthplace of La Movida Madrileña, this alternative district is still cutting edge today

CENTRO
Get a serious dose of history with the magnificent Plaza Mayor and Puerta del Sol

LAVAPIÉS
Cutting-edge art galleries and ground-breaking theatre in this artistic quarter

LA LATINA
Head here for Sunday brunch in Plaza de la Paja with Madrid's beautiful people

RECOLETOS
Home to the city's best museums, fountains, statues and the elegant Retiro park

For a full description of each neighbourhood,
including the places you really must not miss, see the Introduction